AESTHETIC THEORY

AESTHETIC THEORY

Matthew Manus

iUniverse, Inc.
New York Lincoln Shanghai

AESTHETIC THEORY

iUniverse, Inc.

For information address:
iUniverse, Inc.
2021 Pine Lake Road, Suite 100
Lincoln, NE 68512
www.iuniverse.com

ISBN: 0-595-32627-7

Printed in the United States of America

Contents

Introduction

My aesthetic theory was developed in isolation from other art theorists. This aesthetic theory is my contribution to the perception of art and art history.

Matthew Manus
July 2004
Saint Louis, MO USA

Alaterality

Alaterality is the idea that the artwork is unbounded and is integrated with the environment in which it is positioned.

Anaconstruction

Anaconstruction describes the process by which aesthetic movements return into popular fashion after decades or more of disuse. Anaconstruction likewise describes the process by which older styles are utilized in new and meaningful combinations.

Apexion

Apexion describes the process by which individual artworks become the paradigms of aesthetic movements. For example, "The Wasteland" by T.S. Eliot is generally regarded as the paradigmatic poem of Modernist poetry.

Arithmation

Arithmation is the idea that there are a finite number of elements that are utilized in the production of an artwork.

Bioconstruction

Bioconstruction describes the process by which an artwork influences the viewer's aesthetic in regards to everyday life.

Chronoconstruction

Chronoconstruction describes the process by which an artwork and the legacy of an artist assume variant positions in the art world and the academy over the course of time.

Contraconstruction

Contraconstruction describes the process by which many aesthetic movements of the twentieth century avant-garde intentionally created opposition to their artwork in order to generate publicity.

Decretion

Decretion describes the process by which the creation of an artwork resolves an intellectual problem for the artist.

Ekation

Ekation is the idea that an artwork contains unknown elements of meaning that neither the artist nor the viewer is aware of.

Epiconstruction

Epiconstruction describes the process by which aesthetic works and perceptions are built upon previous aesthetic works and perceptions.

Geopoeisis

Geopoisis describes the process by which an artwork integrates itself with the global imagination. For example, many of M.C. Escher's paintings have become part of the world's store of imagery, and can be seen on many things, ranging from posters to clothing.

Implicarition

Implicarition describes the idea that art movements often overlap each other and can often be synchronous with each other.

Ipseconstruction

Ipseconstruction describes the process by which the artist develops his/her own aesthetic and utilizes his/her aesthetic in the production of artworks.

Law of Position

The law of position states that the position of the artwork in relation to the viewer affects the way in which the artwork is perceived.

Ludation

Ludation describes the process by which the artist plays with ideas and intellectual problems in the composition of an artwork.

Magnifaction

Magnifaction describes the process by which an artwork becomes known as 'great'. Likewise, magnifaction describes the process by which the artist becomes known to the general public.

Mirability

Mirability describes the relationship between the viewer and the artwork. The interrelationship between the viewer and the artwork is one of the ways in which the artwork's meaning is generated in the mind of the viewer.

Multiconstruction

Multiconstruction describes the total environment that an artwork creates simply by existing, for example, the literature the artwork generates through criticism, as well as the commercial value of the artwork in the global market.

Mundation

Mundation describes the process by which the artwork becomes part of the art world and how the artwork takes its position in relation to other artworks within the art world.

Phasion

Phasion is the idea that the artist creates a new aesthetic in each new artwork.

Pheration

Pheration is the idea that the artist brings the entirety of his/her experience to the artwork, as does the viewer in the act of viewing.

Polylogics

Polylogics describes the idea that the process of artistic creation and the process of aesthetic perception involve many different logics that coexist simultaneously in the process of artistic composition and the act of viewing.

Praefinition

Praefinition is the idea that the viewer approaches the artwork with a predetermined aesthetic.

Speculition

Speculition describes the process by which the artist imagines the artwork in his/her mind, in many cases before engaging in the production of the artwork. Speculition likewise describes the process by which the artwork is brought into being by the artist based upon the conceptions of the artwork that obtain in the artist's intellect and imagination.

Subconstruction

Subconstruction describes the process by which artists and artworks that are not part of the art world are influenced by the art world to create new artworks, styles and communities.

Supergerity

Supergerity describes the idea that the artist essentially 'feels' quantities in the composition of the artwork.

Telarchy

Telarchy is the idea that the personality of the artist governs the manner in which the artwork is produced and, to an extent, perceived.

Urconstruction

Urconstruction describes the process by which the artist reifies the original mental conception of the artwork.

Verationality

Verationality describes the process by which art critics and art theorists, as well as art viewers, attempt to extract the true meaning or meanings from an artwork. The disparity of verationalities leads inevitably towards disagreement as to what is true, and has thus resulted in both pluralism and the post-modern ethos.

Veterationality

Veterationality describes the process by which works of art that are older than other works of art are regarded by many viewers as having a greater degree of status within the art world than artworks that were produced in recent times.

Vitation

Vitation describes the process by which an artwork becomes a living entity sustained in the mind of the viewer. The artwork, over time, often recombines with other artworks to form new artworks. Vitation likewise describes the process by which the viewer shares in the meaning of an artwork.

Drawings

0-595-32627-7